The Priority Method for Korean ESL Students:
Consonants and Vowels

by

Bradley S. Tice

DISSERTATION.COM

Boca Raton

The Priority Method for Korean ESL Students: Consonants and Vowels

Dissertation.com
Boca Raton, Florida
USA • 2007

ISBN: 1-58112- 361-2
13-ISBN: 978-1-58112-361-6

The Priority Method evolved from first and second language acquisition theories and child language development. Its significant variation from all previous SLA, second language acquisition, pedogogy is that it concentrates on areas of weakness, prioritizing areas of transitional errors from the L1, the first language, to the L2, the second language, that are common in the phonetic performance and production of the ESL student and focuses on the key areas that have significant sociolinguistic and linguistic effects on the ESL student. Why prioritize errors over other aspects of second language learning? Because errors are the significant areas where the students self-confidence and progress come into play.

Because negative aspects of either or both of the above will impede and stigmatize the ESL student and can be a major factor in having the student quit. Many errors are common to each ESL language group giving that group a preliminary map of errors that can be expected before the student arrives at that point. The specific phonetic area covered will be common consonant errors in the ESL student. An abstract of The Priority Method is in the appendix section of this text.

Chapter 1

History

The study of a second or 'foreign language' is by no means a modern phenomena as man has almost always needed or desired the tools of communication with other men and as man has expanded beyond his local boundaries the need to acquire the knowledge and use of a 'new tongue' pushed him into language learning. The ancient Greeks used the study of language as a tool for rhetorical practice. The first world language in the western hemisphere was Latin but by the Seventeenth Century it had failed from regular use and became a dead language. The study of Latin was used through the Nineteenth Century as a tool to study grammar and rhetoric as a foreign language and was thought that the study of Latin was an end in itself as it was for developing the intellect rather than a vehicle for communication.

The modern languages, French, Spanish and German, began to enter the curriculum in the Eighteenth Century and as with the study of Latin was learned by route with little stress on oral practice. By the Nineteenth Century this form of foreign language study had become standard being codified with rules and became known as the Grammar-Translation Method and was in use to the Nineteen Forties. A school of dissent arose during the Mid-Nineteenth century which questioned the validity of the Grammar-Translation Method. Such men as C. Marcel, 1793-1896, modeled language learning on that of children and stressed the importance of meaning in language and F. Gouin, 1831-1896, also a Frenchman, who believed that a language must be taught with a clear context of meaning reinforced by an action or event.

Far from the static Grammar-Translation Method, the Gouin series was a physical, interactive way of language learning. It was during the later part of the Nineteenth Century that the study of Phonetics, the scientific analysis and description of sound systems of languages, was used to reorient language as primarily a spoken rather than a written system of communication. During this time a new school of thought arose proposing that the second language was learned like the first language. This 'natural method' of language learning would in turn lead to the Direct Method.

The Direct Method popularized the natural method in France and Germany while a Swiss, L. Sauveur, 1826-1907, and a German, Maximilian Berlitiz opened successful commercial schools in the United States. The principles of the method was instruction conducted in the target language and practical sentences and vocabulary where taught. Although popular in Europe England had its own school of thought developed from studies starting in the Nineteen Twenties. Two British applied linguists Harold Palmer and A.S. Hornby developed a methodology that involved systematical principles of selection, gradation and presentation.

This system was referred to as the Oral Approach and although used oral emphasis like the Direct Method, was systematic in theory and practice. America would finally add to the language learning studies in the Nineteen Fifties primarily from the behaviorist school of psychology and what would be called structural linguistics. The behaviorist theories on language learning where than children are born with general learning potential, that behavior is shaped by reinforcement of particular responses to particular stimuli and that learning occurs entirely through environment. The structural linguists viewed language as a system of structurally related elements for encoding meaning. These elements would be phonemes, morphemes, words and sentence types. The emphases was on oral. A child learns to speech before it can read or write and speech is the 'priority' in language teaching as it is the 'priority' in language learning.

The Audiolingual method enjoyed popularity late into the next decade but it was the publication of Syntactic Structures in Nineteen Fifty Seven by MIT linguistics professor Noam Chomsky that brought into question the validity of many of structural linguistics principles of language processing and acquisition. Chomsky questioned why the structural linguists could not account for the creative aspect of individual sentences, many that are grammatically unsound yet convey meaning. Although Chomsky was not interested in applied second language acquisition, he would stay with theoretical linguistics and his theory of 'universal grammar' that proposed innate systems in the human brain that function as language processors, he did open the door for what would be called Communicative Language Teaching.

The theory behind Communicative Language Teaching is that language is primarily communication and that meaning in language is paramount. This brief history of language learning emphases two points, that language learning has evolved from mechanical to spoken and that despite all the theories and applications on language learning, people still learn to communicate regardless, and at times , inspite of them.

Although there is little concensus about the exact origins of the Korean language, two schools of thought have developed over the years to explain the origins of this language. The Southern view holds two theories. The first is that the Korean language is related to the Davidian languages of India and the second that it is related to the Austronesian languages of Polynesia. The Northern view has Korean related to the Altaic family of languages such as Turkic and Mongolian. There are two official dialects existing in modern Korea. The Seoul dialect in South Korea and the Phyong'yang dialect in North Korea.

and the hard palate is the roof of the mouth. The alveolar ridge is behind the upper teeth, also a part of the articulatory process, and next to the hard palate. The timing, placement and overall movement of articulators determine the sharpness and clarity of production.

Chapter 4

Phonetics

Phonetics is the study of sounds when speaking. The smallest unit of sound is the phoneme. These phonemes are grouped together in what is called the phonemic system. These phonemes are represented as symbols of the sound and are written as a phonemic transcription. Phonology is the study of how these phonemes interact with each other as syllables. Other aspects of phonology are stress and intonation.

Stress is the relative strength of the syllable and intonation is the pitch of the voice to imply meaning. The vocal tract is the region which is between the larynx and the mouth and nostrils and is made up of various parts called articulators. Correct placement of these articulators during pronunciation are crucial to the accurate production of the target language sound. Because of this each phoneme is depicted by a diagram of a human head depicting the correct placement of the articulators for each phoneme.

Chapter 5

Errors

A consonant is a sound produced with an obstruction in the oral cavity. Traditional Korean ESL consonant trouble areas are: [p], [b], [t], [d], [k], [g], [f], [v], [θ], [ð], [h], [š], [ž], [s], [z], [c], [j], [m], [n], [ŋ], [l], [r], [w], and [y].

[p] as in 'spot'.

Substitution error.

[p] will be substituted by [p']

[b] as in '<u>b</u>et'.

Substitution error.

[b] will be a problem in the final release and will be substituted by [ɪ].

[t] as in 'st_op'.

Substitution error.

[t] will be substituted by [tʰ].

[d] as in '<u>d</u>ay'.

Substitution error.

[d] will be a problem in the final release position and will be substituted by [ɪ].

20

[k] as in 'skate'.

Substitution error.

[k] will be substituted in final aspiration position by [kʰ].

[g] as in 'good'.

Substitution error.

[g] will be a problem in the final release position and will be substituted by [王].

[f] as in 'fat'.

Substitution error.

[f] will be substituted by [p].

[v] as in 'vat'.

Substitution error.

[v] will be substituted by [f].

[θ] as in 'th̲in'.

Substitution error.

[θ] will be substituted by [s].

[ð] as in 'then'.

Substitution error.

[ð] will be substituted by [d].

[h] as in 'hat'.

Substittution error.

[h] will be confused by the voiceless vowel as in 'idea'.

[s] as in 'sit'.

Substitution error.

[s] will be substituted in the final position by [ɪ].

[z] as in 'zoo'.

Substittution error.

[z] will be substittuted by [s].

[s̈] as in '<u>sh</u>ed'.

Substitution error.

[s̈] will be substituted in the final position by ⊞.

[ʒ] as in 'measure'.

Substitution error.

[ʒ] will be substittuted by [j].

[c] as in 'chain'.

Substitution error.

[c] will be substituted in the final position by [i].

[j] as in 'range'.

Substitution error.

[j] will be substituted in the final position by [i].

[m] as in 'met'.

Substitution error.

[m] will be substituted by [m·].

[n] as in 'net'.

Substitution error.

[n] will be substituted by [n̥].

[ŋ] as in 'ki<u>ng</u>'.

Substitution error.

[ŋ] will be substituted by [ŋ·].

[l] as in 'link'.

Substitution error.

[l] will be substituted by [n].

[r] as in 'red'.

Substitution error.

[r] will be substituted by [n].

[w] as in 'wish'.

Substitution error.

[w] will be substituted in the final position by [u].

[y] as in 'yes'.

Substitution error.

[y] will be substituted in the final position by [i] and [ɪ].

Chapter 6

Pedogogy

Because of the inherent difficulties of SLA, Second Language Acquistion, students detecting phonetic errors in their own speech due to the fact that they do not hear foreign language phonemes, only that of their own, and will not readily improve in that area of pronunciation unless a model of the correct way can be understood and produced. These problems can be magnified if the instructors pronunciation is not that of the target language, producing a vicious cycle of incorrect pronunciation of English.

To aid in the learning of correct pronunciation the student must recognize a new pattern of speech on the bases of differences between native and target languages. The process of this recognition is by way of having the student listen to a tape of a model of the target language with its fidelity of production, rhythm and intonation. When the student has a conceptual grasp of the English sound pattern, then the second stage of the process begins.

The best method of learning to pronounce correctly is to have an accurate model from which to compare the students pronunciation too. This is obtained by using the Language Learning Loop. What the Language Learning Loop entails is the use of two tape recorders, one as input and the other as output. The input tape is to be used with a specific pronunciation tape that allows for time intervals between prerecorded segments that allows the student to practice the pronunciation of the target language. The output tape recorder is monitoring and recording both the students pronunciation and also the input tapes lessons, that are played via a loud speaker system, so that the student may analyze both the model pronunciation as well as their own, giving the student a point of reference from which to work. The tape will follow the Priority Method workbook and will allow the student to reinforce pronunciation practice with that of specific writing skills, dictation, that will reinforce the spelling of the phonetic model, adding to the exposure of the target language.

The method of the pedogogy will be listening first, pronunciation practice second and then listening, pronunciation and simple writing exercises third to reinforce the concept of the phonetic model. The workbook is laid out in progressive segments each starting with a specific phonetic sound and then incorporating it into a word and then a sentence. The reason for this is to give the student an understanding of the phonetic sound alone, a condition that usually only occurs with vowels, and then a more realistic practice that incorporates stress and tone in the use of a word or sentence. By applying this systematic introduction to the phonetic sound and its application in words and sentences, the student will be able to practice model pronunciation in the target language.

Chapter 7

Consonants

Consonant sounds in the English sound pattern are: [p], [b], [t], [d], [k], [g], [s], [z], [f], [v], [ʃ], [ʒ], [h], [Ɵ], [ð], [l], [r], [w], [j], [m], [n], [ŋ], [tʃ] and [dʒ].

[p] as in peanut.

Description of production of sound.   Lips are closed and the nasal
passage is blocked by the soft palate.   Forcing the unvocalized air
from the lungs into the mouth.   Quickly flip the lips open and expel
the air out in one motion.   The resulting sound should be [p] as in
peanut.

Description of articulators in diagram.   The lips are closed and the
tongue is resting slightly away from lower set of front teeth.   There
maybe a thrusting of the tip of the tongue when air is expelled
against the lower set of teeth.

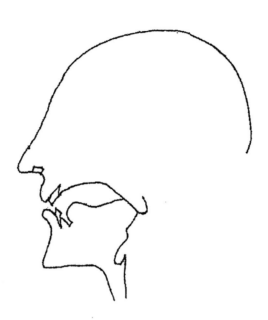

[b] as in beat.

Description of production of sound. The lips are closed and pressure is built up and expelled through unrounded lips. The sound is voiced and should sound like [b] as in beat.

Description of articulators in diagram. Lips are held together and tongue is slightly away from the lower set of front teeth. Flip the lips outward and expel the air that is voiced.

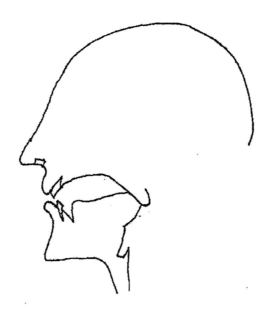

50

[t] as in tom.

Description of production of sound. The tip of the tongue is placed against the upper alveolar ridge behind the front teeth. The lips are open and air is expelled suddenly between the tongue and the hard palate. The sound is voiceless. The resulting sound should be [t] as in tom.

Description of articulators in diagram. The lips are open and the tip of the tongue is against the upper alveolar ridge behind the front teeth. Holding the air behind the tongue and the hard palate drop the tip of the tongue and expel the air through this passage.

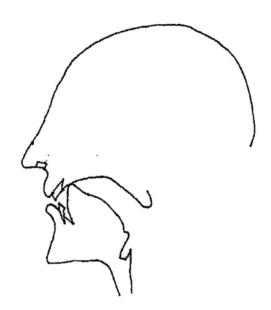

52

[d] as in dot.

Description of production of sound. The lips are open and the tip of the tongue is against the upper alveolar ridge of the front teeth. The air is expelled between the tongue and the hard palate and the sound is voiced. The resulting sound is [d] as in dot.

Description of articulators in diagram. The lips are open and unrounded and the tip of the tongue is against the upper alveolar ridge behind the front teeth. Holding the air behind the tongue and the hard palate lower the tip of the tongue and expel the voiced sound.

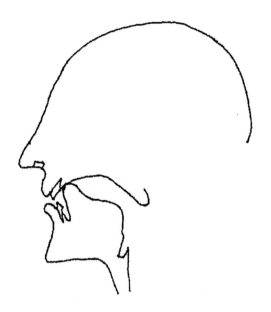

[k] as in <u>k</u>ick.

Description of production of sound. The lips are open and unrounded.
The soft palate, velum, is blocking the nasal passage and the tongue is
placed against the soft palate. Building up pressure in the mouth
lower the tongue and expel the air out. The result should sound like
[k] as in kick.

Description of articulators in diagram. The lips are open and the back
of the tongue is against the soft palate building up pressure in the
back of the mouth. Lower the tongue and expel the air.

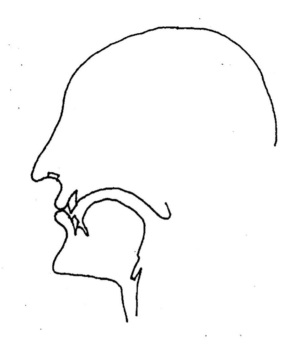

56

[g] as in great.

Description of production of sound. The lips are open and the back of the tongue is resting against the soft palate. A light amount of pressure is built up and expelled softly by the lowering of the tongue. The sound is voiced. The result should sound like [g] as in great.

Description of articulators in diagram. The mouth and lips are open. The back of the tongue is resting against the soft palate and slight amount of air pressure is built up. The tongue is lowered and the air is expelled softly.

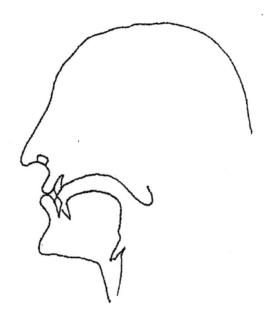

[s] as in sell.

Description of production of sound. The lips are open and sound is produced by simultaneously blocking the nasal passage with the soft palate, velum, and bring the tongue near the back of the upper set of front teeth. The front of the tongue is grooved and does not touch either the sides or the middle of the teeth. The air is expelled through the front groove of the tongue and the alveolar ridge and front teeth. The result should sound like [s] as in sell.

Description of articulators in the diagram. The lips are open and unrounded. The nasal passage is blocked by the velum and the tip of the tongue is near the upper alveolar ridge behind the front teeth. The front of the tongue is grooved and does not touch either the sides or the middle of the teeth. Air is expelled through the groove in the front of the tongue and the alveolar ridge and front teeth.

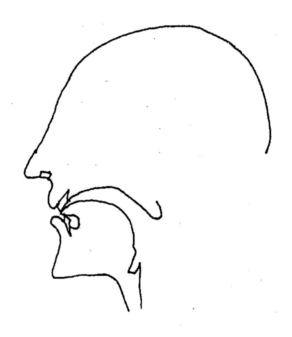

60

[z] as in zoo.

Description of production of sound. The lips are open and unrounded. The nasal passage is blocked by the velum and the tip of the tongue is near the upper alveolar ridge behind the front teeth. The front of the tongue is grooved and does not touch either the sides or the middle of the teeth. Expel air through the front groove in the tongue and the upper alveolar ridge and front teeth. The sound is voiced. The result should sound like [z] as in zoo.

Description of articulators in diagram. The lips are open and unrounded. The nasal passage in back is blocked by the velum and the tip of the tongue is near the upper alveolar ridge behind the front teeth. The front of the tongue is grooved and does not touch either sides or the middle of the teeth. Expel voiced air through the front groove of the tongue and upper alveolar ridge and front teeth.

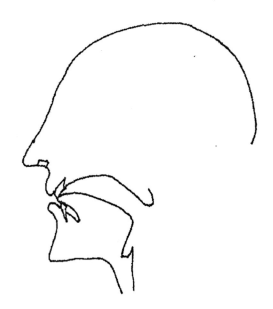

[f] as in fat.

Description of production of sound. The lips and teeth have a narrow opening and the nasal passage is blocked with the soft palate. The upper set of front teeth are resting on the back half of the lower lip. A stream of air is forced through the narrow opening between the lips and teeth. The sound is unvoiced. The result should sound like [f] as in fat.

Description of articulators in diagram. The lips and teeth have a narrow opening and the nasal passage is blocked with the soft palate. The upper set of front teeth are resting on the back half of the lower lip. A stream of air is forced through the narrow opening between the lips and teeth.

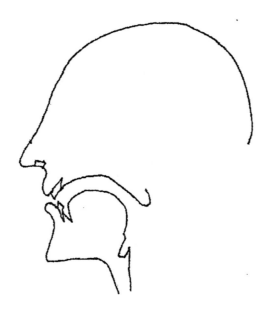

[v] as in voice.

Description of production of sound. The lips and teeth have a narrow opening and the nasal passage is blocked by the soft palate and the upper front teeth are resting on the back half of the lower lips. A stream of air is forced through a narrow gap in the lips and teeth. The sound is voiced. The result should sound like [v] as in voice.

Description of articulators in diagram. The lips and teeth have a narrow opening and the nasal passage is blocked by the soft palate and the upper front teeth are resting on the back half of the lower lips. A stream of air is forced through a narrow gap in the lips and teeth.

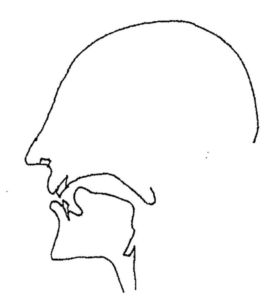

[ʃ] as in she.

Description of production of sound. The lips are open and slightly rounded. The nasal passage is blocked with soft palate and the blade of the tongue is flat and near the upper alveolar ridge behind the front teeth. Force the air stream through the opening between the tongue and upper alveolar ridge behind the front teeth. The sound is unvoiced. The result should sound like [ʃ] as in she.

Description of the articulators of the diagram. The lips are open and slightly rounded. The nasal passage is blocked with the soft palate and the ball of the tongue is flat and near the upper alveolar ridge behind the front teeth. Force the air stream through the opening between the tongue and upper alveolar ridge behind the front teeth.

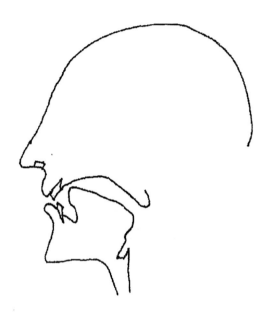

[ʒ] as in treasure.

Description of production of sound. The lips are open and slightly rounded. The nasal passage is blocked with the soft palate and the blade of the tongue is flat and near the upper alveolar ridge behind the front teeth. Force the air stream through the opening between the tongue and the alveolar ridge behind the front teeth. The sound is voiced. The result should sound like [ʒ] as in treasure.

Description of articulators in the diagram. The lips are open and slightly rounded. The nasal passage is blocked with the soft palate and the blade of the tongue is flat and near the upper alveolar ridge behind the front teeth. Force the air stream through the opening between the tongue and the alveolar ridge behind the front teeth.

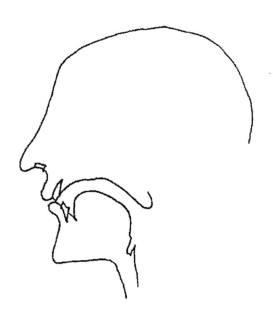

[h] as in hot.

Description of production of sound. The mouth and lips are wide open.
The tongue is laying on the floor of the mouth. Expel a quick burst of
air from the lungs. The sound is voiceless. The result should sound
like [h] as in hot.

Description of articulators of the diagram. The mouth and lips are
wide open. The tongue is laying on the floor of the mouth. Expel a
quick burst of air from the lungs.

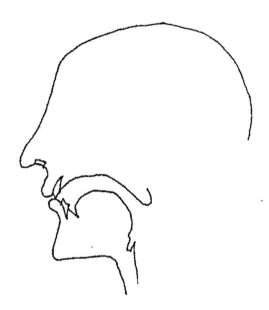

[Θ] as in <u>th</u>ank.

Description of production of sound. The lips are parted and unrounded. The nasal passage is blocked with the soft palate. The blade of the tongue is resting against the upper molars and the tip of the tongue is touching the backs of the upper and lower back sides of the front teeth. Forcing a stream of air between the upper front teeth and the tongue tip. The sound is unvoiced. The result should sound like [Θ] as in thank.

Description of articulators in the diagram. The lips are parted and unrounded. The nasal passage is blocked with the soft palate. The blade of the tongue is resting against the upper molars and the tip of the tongue is touching the backs of the upper and lower back sides of the front teeth. Forcing a stream of air between the upper front teeth and the tongue tip. The sound is unvoiced. The result should sound like [Θ] as in thank.

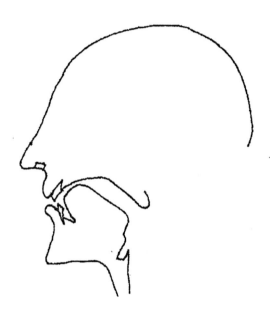

[ð] as in <u>th</u>at.

Description of production of sound. The lips are parted and unrounded. The nasal passage is blocked with the soft palate. The blade of the tongue is resting against the upper molars and the tip of the tongue is touching the backs of the upper and lower back sides of the front teeth. Forcing a stream of air between the upper front teeth and vibrating the tongue tip. The sound is voiced. The result should sound like [ð] as in that.

Description of produced sound. The lips are parted and unrounded. The nasal passage is blocked with the soft palate. The blade of the tongue is resting against the upper molars and the tip of the tongue is touching the backs of the upper and lower back sides of the front teeth. Forcing a stream of air between the upper front teeth and vibrating the tongue tip.

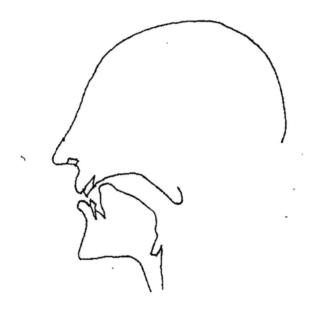

[l] as in long.

Description of production of sound. The lips are open and the tip of the tongue is against the hard palate of the mouth. Expel a stream of air over both sides of the tongue. The sound is voiced. The result should sound like [l] as in long.

Description of articulators of diagram. The lips are open ant the tip of the tongue is against the hard palate of the mouth. Expel a stream of air over both sides of the tongue.

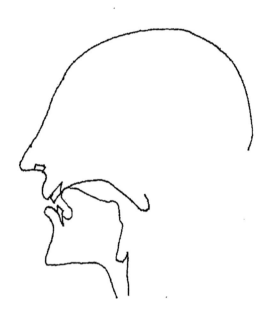

[r] as in rat.

Description of production of sound. Lips are slightly apart and unrounded. The tip of the tongue is arched slightly back and away from the upper alveolar ridge. The sides of the tongue are touching the upper alveolar ridge and teeth. The sound is voiced. The result should sound like [r] as in rat.

Description of articulators in the diagram. Lips are slightly apart and unrounded. The tip of the tongue is arched slightly back and away from the upper alveolar ridge. The sides of the tongue are touching the upper alveolar ridge and teeth.

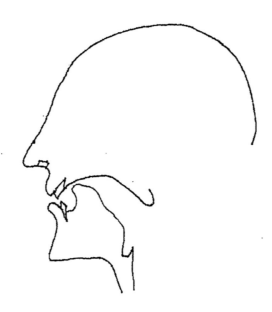

[w] as in well.

Description of production of sound. Lips are rounded and the back of the tongue is raised in the back of the mouth. The vocalized air is expelled through the hole in the rounded lips. The resulting sound is [w] as in well.

Description of articulators in the diagram. The lips are rounded. The back of the tongue is raised in the back section of the mouth. Vocalized air is expelled through the rounded lips.

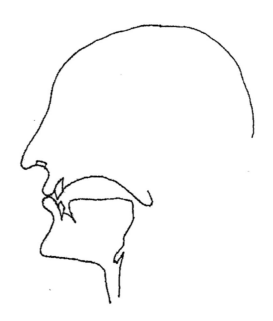

[j] as in jar.

Description of production of sound. Lips are parted and the tongue is raised into contact with the inner ridge of the upper molars. Vocalized air is expelled between the tongue and the hard palate. The result should sound like [j] as in jar.

Description of articulators in the diagram. The lips are parted and the tongue is raised into contact with the inner ridge of the upper molars.

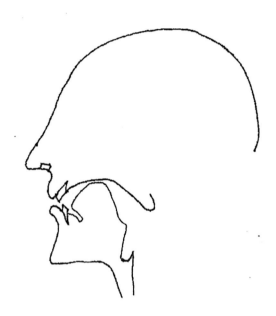

[m] as in <u>m</u>eet.

Description of production of sound. Lips are closed and the tongue is down. Releasing air through the nasal cavity from the throat. The result should sound like [m] as in meet.

Description of articulators in the diagram. The lips are closed and the tongue is down. Air will be released through the nasal cavity from the throat.

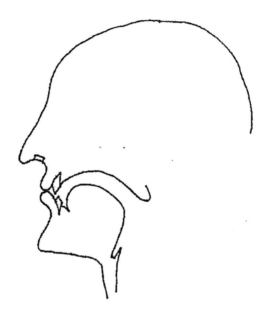

86

[n] as in not

Description of production of sound. Lips are open and the tongue is against the alveolar ridge and inside the upper teeth. The blade of the tongue is against the palate. Air is released from the nasal cavity from the throat. The result should sound like [n] as in not.

Description of articulators in the diagram. The lips are open and the tongue is against the alveolar ridge and inside the upper teeth. The blade of the tongue is against the palate. Air will be released from the nasal cavity from the throat.

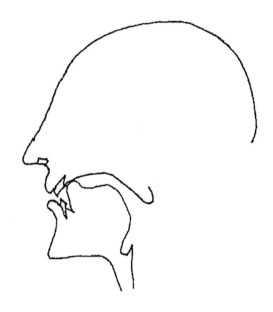

88

[ŋ] as in su<u>n</u>g

Description of production of sound. Lips are open and the back of the
tongue is raised in the back of the mouth against the soft palate.
Release the vocalized air through the nasal cavity from the throat.
The result should sound like [ŋ] as in sung.

Description of articulators in the diagram. The lips are open and the
back of the tongue is raised in the back of the mouth against the soft
palate. Release the vocalized air through the nasal cavity from the
throat.

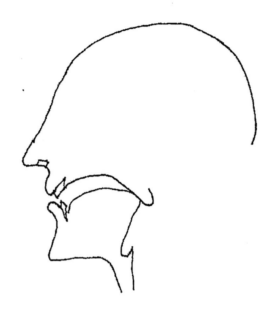

[tʃ] as in <u>ch</u>o p

Description of production of sound. Lips are parted and the tongue is against the alveolar ridge behind the upper teeth. The tongue is pulled down while air is expelled through the constricting lips. The result should sound like [tʃ] as in chop.

Description of articulators in the diagram. The lips are parted and the tongue is against the alveolar ridge behind the upper teeth. The tongue is pulled down while air is expelled through the constricting lips.

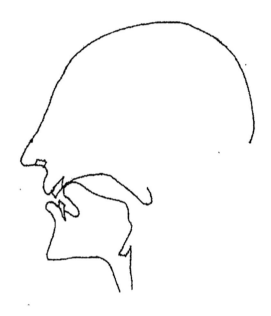

92

[dʒ] as in age

Description of production of sound. The lips are parted and the tongue is behind the upper front teeth. Pull the tongue down and release vocalized air out of the mouth. The result should sound like [dʒ] as in age.

Description of articulators in the diagram. The lips are parted and the tongue is behind the upper front teeth. Pull the tongue down and release vocalized air out of the mouth.

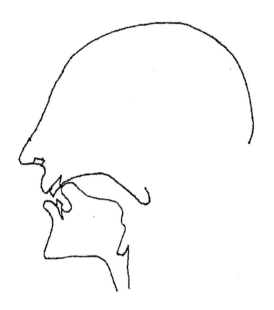

94

Chapter 8

Diagnostic

Even though the Priority Method uses a map of transfer errors that occur from the L1 to the L2, each ESL student will have their own specific errors. Before errors can be corrected they must be realized and diagnosed. This is where diagnostic testing is essential for preliminary evaluation of transfer errors in the ESL student. The diagnostic test consists of a tape recording device, blank tapes and material written in English. The ESL student is to read aloud into the tape recording device the written material, made up of English words and sentences, at a normal cadence. The ESL student will then read the same material aloud at a faster pace and again at a slower pace than normal.

The increase and decrease of reading speed will stress the student and give a more accurate body of data than data at a normal rate of speed alone. Because the readings have a transcript, the original material that was read, there is a correspondence with the recorded material. By playing back the tape of the students English readings, an accurate body of sound production can be evaluated for phonetic quality, stress and intonation. By marking on a copy of the transcript of the material what errors occurred and where those errors occurred within the context of the sound pattern, a detailed analysis of these errors can be deduced. Once a record of these errors is made then the process of correcting them can commence.

Because there is both a record of errors as well as a copy of these errors, the diagnostic tape, these can be used as guide posts for evaluating improvements in the ESL student over time. An important note in choosing English reading material for the diagnostic test. Because the diagnostic test is to test pronunciation rather than competency of reading skills, the material used should be cognitively accessible to the ESL student and relatively comfortable to read aloud at a normal rate of speed.

Summary

The major emphases of the Priority Method is the prioritizing of common transitional errors in ESL students. Efficiency, speed and accuracy are all the results of utilizing the Priority Method. The Priority Method allows for efficient removal of pronunciation errors in all ESL students and although allows for a clear and logical progression for the student to follow, it is of little use if the ESL student does not follow the instructions or make an attempt to constantly analyze their speech and listening skills away from the lessons. Only by continuous practice and awareness can the methods employed by the Priority Method serve to aid the ESL student in improving their speech.

Appendix

Pacific Language Institute
P.O. Box 2214
Cupertino, CA 95015-2214

Bradley S. Tice
Director

An Abstract of The Priority Method
on the Phonetics of the ESL Student

The Priority Method evolved from theories from first and second language acquisition and child language development. Along with error analysis theories , technical advances in equipment have allowed the Priority Method to offer a complete language diagnostic, analysis and training format. Its significant variation from all previous SLA pedagogy is that it concentrates on areas of weakness, prioritizing common areas of transitional errors from L1 to L2 , that commonly occur in the phonetic production and delivery of the ESL student , and focuses on the key areas that have significant sociolinguistic and linguistic effects on the ESL student. Why priorities errors over other aspects of second language learning? Because errors are the significant areas where the student's self confidence and progress come into play. Because negative aspects in any or all of the above will impede and/or stigmatize the ESL student and can be a major factor in having the student quit.

Many errors are common to each ESL language group, giving that group a preliminary map of errors that can be expected before the student arrives at that point. The specific phonetic area covered will be common consonant and vowel errors in the ESL student. There will be a text, work book and a tape of which the work book and tape will interact with each other using the Priority Method and a Learning Loop. The Learning Loop is a term that describes the learning system used to facilitate the correct recognition and production of the English sound pattern. It uses two tape recorders of which one is to play the tape with the exercises on it of a Model of English pronunciation. The second tape recorder is recording both the Model pronunciation and the students attempt to duplicate the Model English sound pattern. Because the student hears only those sound patterns that are similar or the same to their L1 language the need to compare their L2 production of English with that of a Model of English will result in a more accurate diagnosis. The potential of this method as a supplement to any language course or program is great as it can be used with any language group and at any level of learning.

The Priority Method

Bradley S. Tice

The Priority Method is a three step system designed to evaluate, diagnose, and correct phonemic transfer errors from the L1 to the L2 in SLA, Second Language Acquisition, students and will focus on Polish students learning ESL. The term Priority Method was used because the process prioritizes phonemic transfer errors over other aspects of the sound system and deals only with those aspects of the sound pattern that are alien to the SLA student's L1. The reason for this is two fold as, (a) why spend time with all of the sound pattern when only a fraction will be effected, and (b) by focusing on only those areas of weakness in the overall sound pattern, the transfer errors, a more efficient use of time and energy can be spent on correcting these errors.

By decreasing the overall time of acquiring this aspect of pronunciation, the motivation to learn the new language will be high as correct pronunciation will promote an increase in the use of the spoken L2, (George: 1972), and this builds a strong foundation for future rewards in learning the L2.

Step One

The first step of The Priority Method is the evaluation of transfer errors that occur from the L1 to the L2 in SLA students and is done by the use of Contrastive Analysis. This hypothesis proposed by Lado in 1957, (Felix:1980), maintains that the L2 is acquired by these elements most similar to the L1. Thus those elements that are similar from the L1 to the L2 will provide a common phonemic map of transfer errors. This is the theory behind the use of contrastive analysis. The content of the language problems are the transfer errors from the L1 to the L2. The phonology of the SLA student is used as a bases from which a phonemic evaluation of the L2 can take place. From this evaluation, a common distribution of errors is made and can be the starting point of error correction. The use of Contrastive Analysis as a preliminary map of transfer errors is a solid foundation from which to build a general map of transfer errors as the L1 has influence on the L2 as confirmed by Dulay, Burt and Krashen (1982). Because each SLA student is different, individual testing of their respect sound pattern quality is done by the use of Error Analysis.

Step Two

The second part of the Priority Method is the use of Error

Analysis as a diagnostic system used to identify all sound pattern errors, including phonological ones, but is used in this case to expose phonemic transfer errors in SLA students. The SLA student is given a brief, one page, sample text written in the L2 and is to read this text aloud into a tape recording device. The sample text is designed to test the SLA student's level of pronunciation and is not a reading test. The sample text should be read with some ease by the student to make the use of such an L2 text valid. The tape can then be played to diagnose all sound pattern errors and used against the sample text for reference. The sample text and tape recording should be saved for future reference in evaluating the student's pronunciation performance as the same sample text should be used as a control factor in these diagnostic tests.

Step Three
   The third and final step of The Priority Method is the correction of these pronunciation errors evaluated and diagnosed in steps one and two of The Priority Method. This process is done with the use of a Language Learning Loop which is the incorporation of an input-output system of language feedback. Two tape recorders are used of which the (a) tape recorder is playing a model of the L2 sound pattern while, simultaneously,

the (b) tape recorder is recording both the model L2 sound and the pronunciation attempts by the SLA student to model their sound pattern quality with that of the (a) tape recorder model of sound of the L2.

This closed system of communication, as described by Shannon and Weaver (1949), is designed to give the SLA student viable feedback in the manner of ideal pronunciation, the (a) tape recording of a model of the L2, and feedback from the SLA student's pronunciation attempts and the model of the L2. The SLA student then has a model to compare and contrast the pronunciation attempts with that of an ideal model of the L2 sound pattern. This process of feedback, Perren and Trim (1971), of the model and student attempt of the L2, especially the sensori-motor process in articulation, is essential in acquiring the correct model of the spoken L2.

Materials
    Materials for The Priority Method are designed around two areas of practice: (a) routinized oral practice that is developed from simple, phoneme, to complex, sentences, and (b) articulation practice with diagrams and explanations. The routinized oral practice is the heart of the process of correction and is used

with the Language Learning Loop to provide feedback and offer comparative and contrastive analysis by the use of a model of the L2. Although the term 'routine' has negative implications in current ESL thinking, see (Richards and Rogers:1986), it is still the most ideal process of training the articulators and hearing of the SLA student. Redundancy, repetition, occurs at three places, (George:1972), in the input model of communication. Redundancy at the information source, when a statement is repeated. The second is the natural redundancy inherent in the code, the repetition in the phonology of a language. And the third redundancy is information already at the information destination.

The information source, speaker, redundancy is done to make the signal, message, clear for the receiver, listener, and that is why it is repeated. The output mode of the process is the reverse of the previous communication model. The listener, once decoded and processed the message, will become the information source with the desired, hopefully, response. This is what the student is evaluated on. Repetition of the information source signal, message, by the student is to facilitate correct pronunciation and usage of the spoken L2.

The material is designed around the hierarchical premise of simple to complex with the phoneme being the smallest unit of sound and the sentence being the most advanced. The SLA student is given a list of L2 words and sentences that incorporate the transfer error phonemes into words and sentences from which to practice the L2 sound pattern. The use of articulation practice to define the physiological processes of pronunciation are done by the use of articulatory diagrams and explained sound stream control. The diagrams of articulators are usually mid-saggital diagrams of human heads exposing ideal articulation points for each sound unit. Explanations of sound stream control, voicing and breath, are also an advantage for the SLA student to know and can be combined with articulation practice.

Samples
     The following are a sample list of transfer errors most likely to be found in Polish ESL students. The transfer errors and substitutions are taken from Swan and Smith (1987), Retman (1961), and Lyra (1962). The bracketed symbols are IPA.
(a) The vowel [a] as in hot will be substituted for [o].
(b) The vowel [ŋ] as in sing will be substituted for [en].
(c) The consonant [t] as in tan will be substituted for [d].
(d) The consonant [h] as in hat will be substituted for [x].

(e) The consonant [k] as in <u>k</u>eep will be substituted for [x].

This is just a sampling of transfer errors and individual student errors may differ. This is why the second step of The Priority Method is designed to access individual errors in SLA students.

Conclusion

The Priority Method offers a systematic process of phonemic transfer evaluation, diagnoses and correction that can be used with all languages and at all levels of second language acquisition. It must be stressed that The Priority Method only deals with phonemic, rather than phonological, properties of sound and is not a phonological method as it does not deal with language stress and intonation.

The Priority Method can be a useful tool in correcting the often lingering effects of phonemic transfer errors that have become a 'characterization' of learning a new language as best depicted in Ross's (1937) literary works. The average duration of The Priority Method if used four times a week one hour each day for three to four months. Once the transfer and individual errors are correct in the SLA student the need for The Priority Method becomes redundant as the method has worked.

References

Dulay, H., Burt, M., & Krashen, S. (1982). Language two. New York:
   Oxford University Press.

Felix, S.W. (1980). Second language development.
   Tubingen: Gunter Narr Verlag.

George, H.V. (1972). Common errors in language learning.
   Massachusetts: Newbury House Publishers.

Lado, R. (1961). Language testing.
   London: Longman.

Lyra, F. (1962). English and polish in contact.
   Unpublished doctoral dissertation, Indiana University.

Perren, G.E., & Trim, J.L.M. (1971). Applications of linguistics.
   Cambridge: Cambridge University Press.

Retman, R. (1961). Predicting difficulties of polish students of
   english and of english students of polish from comparison of
   sequential phonemes in both languages.
   Unpublished master's thesis, Georgetown University.

Richards, J. C., & Rogers, T.S. (1986). Approaches and methods in
   language teaching. Cambridge: Cambridge University Press.

Ross, L.Q. (1937). The education of hyman kaplan. New York:
   Harcourt, Brace and Company.

Shannon, C. & Weaver, W. (1949). The mathematical theory of
   communication. Urbana: University of Illinois Press.

Swan, M., & Smith, B. (1987). Learner english: a teacher's guide to
   interference and other problems. Cambridge: Cambridge
   University Press.

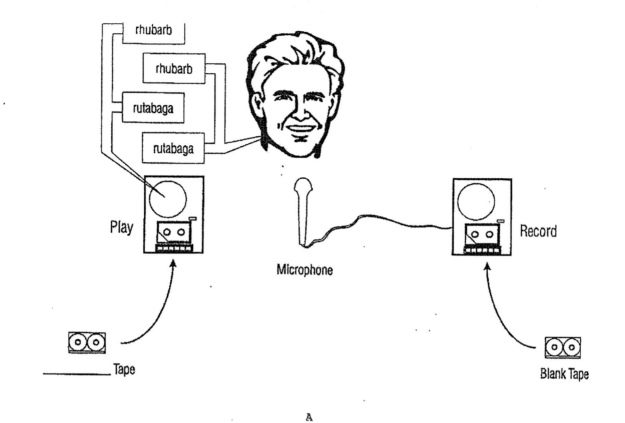

Play

Microphone

Record

Tape

Blank Tape

A

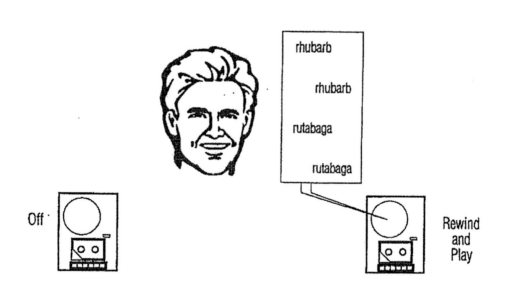

Off

rhubarb

rhubarb

rutabaga

rutabaga

Rewind
and
Play

B

Bradley S. Tice, Director
Pacific Language Institute
P.O. Box 2214
Cupertino, CA 95015-2214
U.S.A.
Business Telephone# (408)253-4449

THE INTERNATIONAL PHONETIC ALPHABET (revised to 1993)

CONSONANTS (PULMONIC)

	Bilabial	Labiodental	Dental	Alveolar	Postalveolar	Retroflex	Palatal	Velar	Uvular	Pharyngeal	Glottal
Plosive	p b			t d		ʈ ɖ	c ɟ	k g	q ɢ		ʔ
Nasal	m	ɱ		n		ɳ	ɲ	ŋ	N		
Trill	ʙ			r					R		
Tap or Flap				ɾ		ɽ					
Fricative	ɸ β	f v	θ ð	s z	ʃ ʒ	ʂ ʐ	ç ʝ	x ɣ	χ ʁ	ħ ʕ	h ɦ
Lateral fricative				ɬ ɮ							
Approximant		ʋ		ɹ		ɻ	j	ɰ			
Lateral approximant				l		ɭ	ʎ	ʟ			

Where symbols appear in pairs, the one to the right represents a voiced consonant. Shaded areas denote articulations judged impossible.

CONSONANTS (NON-PULMONIC)

Clicks		Voiced implosives		Ejectives	
ʘ	Bilabial	ɓ	Bilabial	'	as in:
ǀ	Dental	ɗ	Dental/alveolar	p'	Bilabial
ǃ	(Post)alveolar	ʄ	Palatal	t'	Dental/alveolar
ǂ	Palatoalveolar	ɠ	Velar	k'	Velar
ǁ	Alveolar lateral	ʛ	Uvular	s'	Alveolar fricative

SUPRASEGMENTALS

ˈ	Primary stress	ˌfoʊnəˈtɪʃən
ˌ	Secondary stress	
ː	Long	eː
ˑ	Half-long	eˑ
̆	Extra-short	ĕ
.	Syllable break	ɹi.ækt
ǀ	Minor (foot) group	
‖	Major (intonation) group	
‿	Linking (absence of a break)	

TONES & WORD ACCENTS

LEVEL			CONTOUR		
e̋ or ˥	Extra high		ě or ˇ	Rising	
é ˦	High		ê ˆ	Falling	
ē ˧	Mid		e᷄ ᷄	High rising	
è ˨	Low		e᷅ ᷅	Low rising	
ȅ ˩	Extra low		e᷈ ᷈	Rising-falling	
↓	Downstep		↗	Global rise	etc.
↑	Upstep		↘	Global fall	

VOWELS

Where symbols appear in pairs, the one to the right represents a rounded vowel.

DIACRITICS

Diacritics may be placed above a symbol with a descender, e.g. ŋ̊

̥	Voiceless	n̥ d̥	̤	Breathy voiced	b̤ a̤	̪	Dental	t̪ d̪
̬	Voiced	s̬ t̬	̰	Creaky voiced	b̰ a̰	̺	Apical	t̺ d̺
ʰ	Aspirated	tʰ dʰ	̼	Linguolabial	t̼ d̼	̻	Laminal	t̻ d̻
̹	More rounded	ɔ̹	ʷ	Labialized	tʷ dʷ	̃	Nasalized	ẽ
̜	Less rounded	ɔ̜	ʲ	Palatalized	tʲ dʲ	ⁿ	Nasal release	dⁿ
̟	Advanced	u̟	ˠ	Velarized	tˠ dˠ	ˡ	Lateral release	dˡ
̠	Retracted	i̠	ˤ	Pharyngealized	tˤ dˤ	̚	No audible release	d̚
̈	Centralized	ë	̴	Velarized or pharyngealized	ɫ			
̽	Mid-centralized	ẽ	̝	Raised	e̝ (ɹ̝ = voiced alveolar fricative)			
̩	Syllabic	l̩	̞	Lowered	e̞ (β̞ = voiced bilabial approximant)			
̯	Non-syllabic	e̯	̘	Advanced Tongue Root	e̘			
˞	Rhoticity	ɚ	̙	Retracted Tongue Root	e̙			

OTHER SYMBOLS

ʍ	Voiceless labial-velar fricative	ɕ ʑ	Alveolo-palatal fricatives
w	Voiced labial-velar approximant	ɺ	Alveolar lateral flap
ɥ	Voiced labial-palatal approximant	ɧ	Simultaneous ʃ and x
ʜ	Voiceless epiglottal fricative		Affricates and double articulations can be represented by two symbols joined by a tie bar if necessary.
ʢ	Voiced epiglottal fricative		
ʡ	Epiglottal plosive		k͡p t͡s

Language Learning Loop: A Feedback System

By Dr. Bradley S. Tice
Advanced Human Design
Cupertino, California U.S.A.

The Language Learning Loop is a feedback loop circuit employed to record, evaluate and correct speech sounds of both first and second language learners. The theory behind this system comes from the information sciences, specifically Shannon and Weaver's seminal work "The Mathematical Theory of Communication" published in 1949. Although behaviorism is used to 're-train' the articulators for modification purposes to a target norm of a social ideal of the sound production desired, the system itself is a systems engineering model of a mathematical model of a closed loop system of information signal transfer and modification.

A simple input/ output model of this system will give a general idea of how the language learning loop system functions. The first recording device is playing a model of the ideal sound production of that target language. The second recording device is recording not only the model of ideal production of the target language, but also the attempts of the student to match that target language production by repeating the ideal target models sound delivery (Tice, 1997).

1

From this recording of the model and the attempts to match the model sound production of the target language, a clear and straight-forward recording of the model and attempts of that model can be heard in a comparative and contrastive manner that is necessary for understanding and correction, to achieve the ideal target language production norms. It cannot be understated the importance of this closed loop model of feedback in the diagnosis, evaluation and correction properties this system has to offer the first and second language learning student.

From a systems engineering standpoint, the language learning loop is a self-contained system using existing technologies, tape-recorders, and can be easily implemented into a language laboratory environment, that has been around since the late 1950's, in most language schools or language departments around the world. In other words, this system has a very 'trivial' technology transfer problems inherent in it, and so, can be implemented with little or no costs to a existing language laboratory modules.

The language learning loop will be defined in terms of an information science model and practical aspects of the listening

2

and vocalization pathways will be analyzed for applications to the language learning student.

Diagrams of Language Learning Loop

Figure 1

Source A ⟵———————————⟶ Receiver/Source B

Receiver/Source C

Figure 2

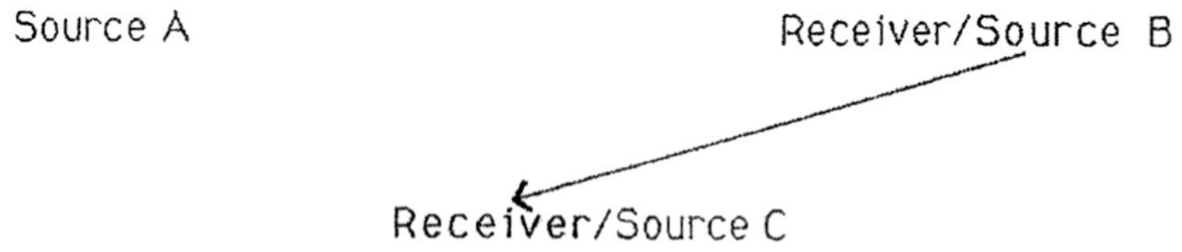

Source A   Receiver/Source B

Receiver/Source C

Figure 3

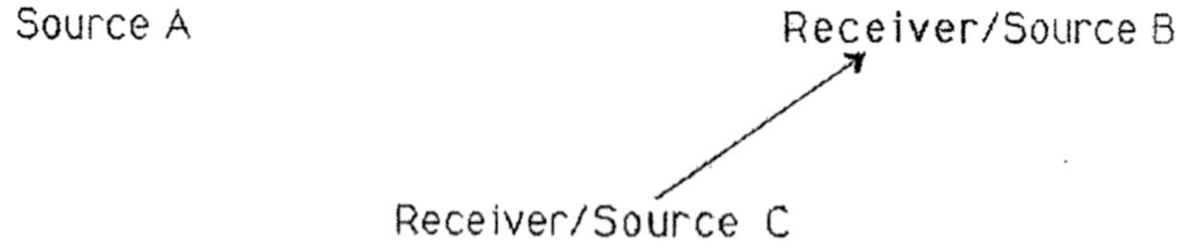

Source A   Receiver/Source B

Receiver/Source C

3

Key to Diagrams

Source A: Output tape recorder playing Target L2 sounds, then followed by spaces for L2 student's attempts to produce the L2 sounds.[1]

Receiver/Source B: Input functions as a receiver, the L2 student listens to the Target L2 sound. Output functions as a source, the L2 student produces an attempt of the L2 sound.

Receiver/ Source C: Input function #1 as a receiver, records Target L2 sound. Input Function #2 as a receiver, records the L2 students attempt to produce the L2 sound. Output functions as a source, play recorded Target L2 and the L2 students attempt to produce the L2 sound.

Note: The goal of this system is the Output mode of the Receiver/Source C as it affords a comparative/contrastive analysis of the L2 sound system.

Information Theory to Language Learning Loop

The communication model for human speech found in Shannon and Weaver's seminal work The Mathematical Theory of

---

[1] L2 is a linguistic notation for second language, i.e. all languages learned after the first language..

4

Communication has for almost 50 years been the bench mark for describing human communication (Shannon and Weaver, 1949). This model is considered the most 'influential' model of communication ever and with the inclusion of a unidirectional arrow, accounts for a feedback system inherent in human communication transmissions (Pearce, 1994: 20). A model of this linear diagram can be found in Figure A.

Figure A

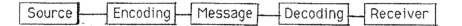

The importance of information theory to the language learning loop is the robustness of the method, in both the mathematical and diagrammatic forms, to explain the system accurately with minimal entropy to the concepts being conveyed. This has been accepted as a standard for the past 50 years and the novelty of such a descriptive system to carry information on complex human behavior and modify and reduce it to a series of arrows and block diagrams, without any major loss of content to the core information base, is still an amazing feature of information theory. Fifty years later and this method of analysis to describe systems is still the paradigm to beat.

5

References

1. Pearce, W.B. <u>Interpersonal Communication: Making Social Worlds</u>. New York: HarperCollins College Publishers, 1994.

2. Shannon, C.E. and Weaver, W. <u>The Mathematical Theory of Communication</u>. Urbana: University of Illinois Press, 1949.

3. Tice, B.S. "Language Learning Loop: A Pronunciation System for Japanese ESL". <u>TESOL MATTERS</u>, Volume 7, Number 2, April/May 1997.

6

Reference

Reference List

1. Comrie, B.(1990). The World's Major Languages.
    Oxford: Oxford University Press.

2. Evans, B W.(1976). Improving Your Speech "Here's How".
    Iowa: Kendall/Hunt Publishing Company.

3. Finegan, E. and N. Besnier.(1989). Language:Its structure and use. New
    York: Harcourt Brace Jovanovich, Publishers.

4. Haycraft, B.(1978). The Teaching of Pronunciation: A Classroom
    Guide. London: Longman.

5. Jung, M.W.(1962). "A Contrastive Study of English and Korean Segmental
    Phonemes with Some Suggestions Toward Pedogogical Application."
    M.S. Georgetown University.

6. Kenworthy, J.(1988).Teaching English Pronunciation.
    London: Longman.

7. Lilly-Cheng, L.R.(1987). Assessing asian language performance.
    Rockville: Aspen Publishers Inc.

8. Lindfors, J. W.(1987).Children's Language and Learning.
    New Jersey: Prentice-Hall, Inc.

9. Richards, J. C. and T.S. Rodgers (1986).Approaches and Methods in
    Language Teaching: A Description and Analysis.
    Cambridge: Cambridge University Press.

10. Roach, P.(1983).English Phonetics and Phonology.
    Cambridge: Cambridge University Press.

11. Swan, M. and B. Smith.(1987).Learner English: A Teacher's Guide to
    Interference and Other Problems. Cambridge: Cambridge University
    Press.

12. Tice, B. (1994, February). The priority method. Conference conducted at
    the 19th Annual CABE in San Jose, California.

13. Tiffany, W. R. and J. Carrel.(1977).Phonetics: Theory and Application..
    New York: McGraw-Hill.

Bradley S. Tice

About the Author

Dr. Tice is Director and Institute Professor of Language and Linguistics at the Pacific Language Institute located in Cupertino, California U.S.A. His primary interest is in language acquisition, bilingualism and aspects of phonology. He is a member of the following organizations: American Chemical Society, American Society for Microbiology, Association for Computing Machinery, I.E.E.E., The American Physical Society, American Institute of Aeronautics and Astronautics, the Committee on Space Research (COSPAR), California Association for Health, Physical Education, Recreation, and Dance, the Rocky Mountain Modern Language Association, and a founding member of The Mars Society. Dr. Tice has had previous affiliations with both the Stanford Linear Accelerator Center, Menlo Park, California U.S.A. and the NASA Ames Research Center, Moffett Field, California U.S.A. Dr. Tice is listed in the 26th edition of Marquis Who's Who in the West, 53rd Edition of Marquis Who's Who in America, and the 16th Edition of Marquis Who's Who in the World. Dr. Tice is also Director and Institute Professor of Chemistry at Advanced Human Design in Cupertino, California U.S.A. and CEO of Tice Pharmaceuticals in San Jose, California U.S.A.

THE PRIORITY METHOD FOR KOREAN ESL STUDENTS

CONSONANTS AND VOWELS

by

BRADLEY SCOTT TICE

submitted in accordance with the requirements

for the degree of

DOCTOR OF LETTERS

in the subject

Teaching

Specializing in English Language Teaching

at the

Saint Clements University

November 1998

THE PRIORITY METHOD
FOR KOREAN ESL STUDENTS

Volume II   Vowels

The Priority Method

Table of Contents

Acknowledgments

I would like to thank Helen Leavy and Lloyd Nygaard for helping me form my ideas into reality and to Mrs. Lucia Vega-Garcia who helped me to develop my ideas for the 1994 Annual CABE Conference in San Jose, California U.S.A. I would also like to thank both of my parents for being such good sports in allowing me time to think and grow.

Preface

The research for this work was done at the Pacific Language Institute

with a special research grant from the Pacific Language Institute.

Introduction

The Priority Method evolved from first and second language acquisition theories and child language development. Its significant variation from all previous SLA, second language acquisition, pedogogy is that it concentrates on areas of weakness, prioritizing areas of transitional errors from the L1, the first language, to the L2, the second language, that are common in the phonetic performance and production of the ESL student and focuses on the key areas that have significant sociolinguistic and linguistic effects on the ESL student. Why prioritize errors over other aspects of second language learning? Because errors are the significant areas where the students self-confidence and progress come into play.

Because negative aspects of either or both of the above will impede and stigmatize the ESL student and can be a major factor in having the student quit. Many errors are common to each ESL language group giving that group a preliminary map of errors that can be expected before the student arrives at that point. The specific phonetic area covered will be common `vowel` errors in the ESL student. An abstract of The Priority Method is in the appendix section of this text.

Chapter 1

History

The study of a second or 'foreign language' is by no means a modern phenomena as man has almost always needed or desired the tools of communication with other men and as man has expanded beyond his local boundaries the need to acquire the knowledge and use of a 'new tongue' pushed him into language learning. The ancient Greeks used the study of language as a tool for rhetorical practice. The first world language in the western hemisphere was Latin but by the Seventeenth Century it had failed from regular use and became a dead language. The study of Latin was used through the Nineteenth Century as a tool to study grammar and rhetoric as a foreign language and was thought that the study of Latin was an end in itself as it was for developing the intellect rather than a vehicle for communication.

The modern languages, French, Spanish and German, began to enter the curriculum in the Eighteenth Century and as with the study of Latin was learned by route with little stress on oral practice. By the Nineteenth Century this form of foreign language study had become standard being codified with rules and became known as the Grammar-Translation Method and was in use to the Nineteen Forties. A school of dissent arose during the Mid-Nineteenth century which questioned the validity of the Grammar-Translation Method. Such men as C. Marcel, 1793-1896, modeled language learning on that of children and stressed the importance of meaning in language and F. Gouin, 1831–1896, also a Frenchman, who believed that a language must be taught with a clear context of meaning reinforced by an action or event.

Far from the static Grammar-Translation Method, the Gouin series was a physical, interactive way of language learning. It was during the later part of the Nineteenth Century that the study of Phonetics, the scientific analysis and description of sound systems of languages, was used to reorient language as primarily a spoken rather than a written system of communication. During this time a new school of thought arose proposing that the second language was learned like the first language. This 'natural method' of language learning would in turn lead to the Direct Method.

The Direct Method popularized the natural method in France and Germany while a Swiss, L. Sauveur, 1826–1907, and a German, Maximilian Berlitiz opened successful commercial schools in the United States. The principles of the method was instruction conducted in the target language and practical sentences and vocabulary where taught. Although popular in Europe England had its own school of thought developed from studies starting in the Nineteen Twenties. Two British applied linguists Harold Palmer and A.S. Hornby developed a methodology that involved systematical principles of selection, gradation and presentation.

This system was referred to as the Oral Approach and although used oral emphasis like the Direct Method, was systematic in theory and practice. America would finally add to the language learning studies in the Nineteen Fifties primarily from the behaviorist school of psychology and what would be called structural linguistics. The behaviorist theories on language learning where than children are born with general learning potential, that behavior is shaped by reinforcement of particular responses to particular stimuli and that learning occurs entirely through environment. The structural linguists viewed language as a system of structurally related elements for encoding meaning. These elements would be phonemes, morphemes, words and sentence types. The emphases was on oral. A child learns to speech before it can read or write and speech is the 'priority' in language teaching as it is the 'priority' in language learning.

The Audiolingual method enjoyed popularity late into the next decade but it was the publication of Syntactic Structures in Nineteen Fifty Seven by MIT linguistics professor Noam Chomsky that brought into question the validity of many of structural linguistics principles of language processing and acquisition. Chomsky questioned why the structural linguists could not account for the creative aspect of individual sentences, many that are grammatically unsound yet convey meaning. Although Chomsky was not interested in applied second language acquisition, he would stay with theoretical linguistics and his theory of 'universal grammar' that proposed innate systems in the human brain that function as language processors, he did open the door for what would be called Communicative Language Teaching.

The theory behind Communicative Language Teaching is that language is primarily communication and that meaning in language is paramount. This brief history of language learning emphases two points, that language learning has evolved from mechanical to spoken and that despite all the theories and applications on language learning, people still learn to communicate regardless, and at times , inspite of them.

Although there is little concensus about the exact origins of the Korean language, two schools of thought have developed over the years to explain the origins of this language. The Southern view holds two theories. The first is that the Korean language is related to Davidian languages of India and the second is that it is related to the Austronesian languages of Polynesia. The Northern view has Korean related to the Altaic family of languages such as Turkic and Mongolian. There are two official dialects existing in modern Korea. The Seoul dialect in South Korea and the Phyong'yang dialect in North Korea.

Chapter 2

Methodology

The Priority Method prioritizes common errors that traditionally occur in the transition from L1 to L2 in the ESL student. The Priority Method's goal is to have the ESL student recognize, understand and produce correctly articulated speech in themselves and in others. Only when the student has obtained these abilities can the manner of the students speech be considered correct.

The student must be able to comprehend the structural details of the sound pattern for it to be perceived, not just the meaning of a word or a sentence, and although good speech form will not substitute for content, it is a given that good form compliments content. Because speech is used by the individual to communicate at a greater frequency than writing, by a factor of over ten to one, the accuracy of pronunciation will greatly aid in the clear delivery of the desired meaning.

Chapter 3

Physiology

There are four stages in the production of sound respiration, phonation, resonation and articulation. The respiratory mechanism includes the diaphragm, the lungs, the bronchi and the trachea. The diaphragm is the main muscle for breathing and is the foundation for tones. The lungs are air sacks that hold a volume of air that is expelled through the bronchi and up the trachea. Air travels through the larynx where the air is modulated and vibrated by the vocal folds and this is where voice is produced. The air is then next given depth and amplitude to make it audible by the use of resonators.

There are six resonators; laryngopharynx, pharynx, oral cavity, nasal cavity, oro-pharynx and naso-pharynx. The main resonators are the mouth and pharynx. Size and shape of these cavities can be modified by adjusting the mandible and the tongue. Sound is next articulated into intelligible sounds by the articulators. There are six articulators; lips mandible, tongue, soft palate, hard palate and alveolar ridge. The lips are used in producing two types of sounds, bilabial sounds when the lips are in contact with each other, and labiodental sounds when lips contact teeth.

Articulation is accomplished by the adjustment of the mandible or jaw and tongue that is divided into five parts beginning with the tip, blade, front, back and root. The soft palate is used to control air from the nasal cavity and the hard palate is the roof of the mouth. The alveolar ridge is behind

the upper teeth, also a part of the articulatory process, and next to the hard

palate. The timing, placement and overall movement of articulators

determine the sharpness and clarity of production.

Chapter 4

Phonetics

Phonetics is the study of sounds when speaking. The smallest unit of sound is the phoneme. These phonemes are grouped together in what is called the phonemic system. These phonemes are represented as symbols of the sound and are written as a phonemic transcription. Phonology is the study of how these phonemes interact with each other as syllables. Other aspects of phonology are stress and intonation.

Stress is the relative strength of the syllable and intonation is the pitch of the voice to imply meaning. The vocal tract is the region which is between the larynx and the mouth and nostrils and is made up of various parts called articulators. Correct placement of these articulators during pronunciation are crucial to the accurate production of the target language sound. Because of this each phoneme is depicted by a diagram of a human head depicting the correct placement of the articulators for each phoneme.

Chapter 5

Errors

A vowel is a sound produced without obstruction in the travel of air from the larynx to the lips. Traditional Korean ESL vowel trouble areas are: [i], [e], [u], [o], [a] and [ə].

[O] as in o̲ff

Substitution error.

[o] will be used for [O].

[o] as in boat.

Substitution error.

[O] will be used for [o].

[ə] as in h<u>u</u>t.

Substitution error.

[I] will be used for [ə].

[i] as in s<u>ee</u>n.

[i] will be absent when in first position of diphthongs.

[ɪ] as in s<u>i</u>t.

[ɪ] will be used before voiceless consonants.

[e] as in d_a_y.

[e] will be used in the first part of diphthongs only.

[ɛ] as in b<u>e</u>t.

[ɛ] will be used before voiceless consonants.

[u] as in d<u>o</u>.

[u] will be substituted in the first part of a word.

[U] as in good.

[U] will be substituted before voiceless consonants.

[a] as in top.

Substitution Error.

[a·] will be used for [a].

Chapter 6

Pedogogy

Because of the inherent difficulties of SLA, Second Language Acquistion, students detecting phonetic errors in their own speech due to the fact that they do not hear foreign language phonemes, only that of their own, and will not readily improve in that area of pronunciation unless a model of the correct way can be understood and produced. These problems can be magnified if the instructors pronunciation is not that of the target language, producing a vicious cycle of incorrect pronunciation of English.

To aid in the learning of correct pronunciation the student must recognize a new pattern of speech on the bases of differences between native and target languages. The process of this recognition is by way of having the student listen to a tape of a model of the target language with its fidelity of production, rhythm and intonation. When the student has a conceptual grasp of the English sound pattern, then the second stage of the process begins.

The best method of learning to pronounce correctly is to have an accurate model from which to compare the students pronunciation too. This is obtained by using the Language Learning Loop. What the Language Learning Loop entails is the use of two tape recorders, one as input and the other as output. The input tape is to be used with a specific pronunciation tape that allows for time intervals between prerecorded segments that allows the student to practice the pronunciation of the target language. The output tape recorder is monitoring and recording both the students pronunciation and also the input tapes lessons, that are played via a loud speaker system, so that the student may analyze both the model pronunciation as well as their own, giving the student a point of reference to work from.

The tape will follow the Priority Method workbook and will allow the student to reinforce pronunciation practice with that of specific writing skills, dictation, that will reinforce the spelling of the phonetic model, adding to the exposure of the target language.

The method of the pedogogy will be listening first, pronunciation practice second and then listening, pronunciation and simple writing exercises third to reinforce the concept of the phonetic model. The workbook is laid out in progressive segments each starting with a specific phonetic sound and then incorporating it into a word and then a sentence. The reason for this is to give the student an understanding of the phonetic sound alone, a condition that usually only occurs with vowels, and then a more realistic practice that incorporates stress and tone in the use of a word or sentence. By applying this systematic introduction to the phonetic sound and its application in words and sentences, the student will be able to practice model pronunciation in the target language.

Chapter 7

Vowels

Vowel sounds in the English sound pattern are: /i/, /I/, /ɑ/, /u/, /ʊ/, /ɔ/, /ɛ/, /ae/, /eI/, /aI/, /ɔI/, /oʊ/, /aʊ/, /ʌ/, /ə/, /ʒ/ and /ʃ/.

/i/ as in k<u>e</u>y

Description of production of sound. Mouth open and lips are parted. Raise the tongue and push it forward in the mouth. The blade of the tongue is arched high in the front of the mouth. The tongue is tense. The resulting sound should be /i/ as in k<u>e</u>y.

Description of articulators in diagram. The mouth is open and the lips are parted. The blade of the tongue is arched high in the front of the mouth. The tongue is tense.

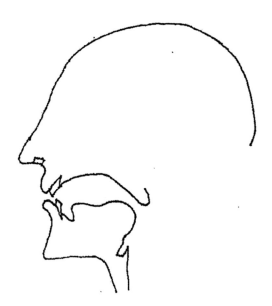

/I/ as in b<u>i</u>t

Description of production of sound. The lips are parted and relaxed and unrounded. The tongue is pushed forward. Expell air over the tongue. The resulting sound should be /I/ as in b<u>i</u>t.

Description of articulators in diagram. The lips are parted and unrounded. The tongue is pushed forward. Expell air over the tongue.

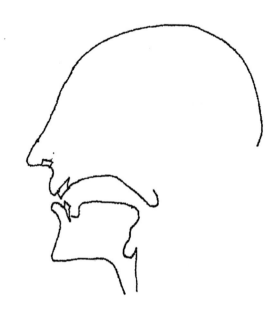

/a/ as in ca̱l m

Description of production of sound. The mouth is open wide and the lips are unrounded. The tongue is low in the mouth with the tip behind the lower front teeth. The tongue muscles are relaxed with the tongue being flat as possible. Vocalized air is expelled out of the mouth. The resulting sound should be /a/ as in ca̱lm.

Description of articulators in diagram. The mouth is open wide and the lips are unrounded. The tongue is low in the mouth with the tip behind the lower front teeth.

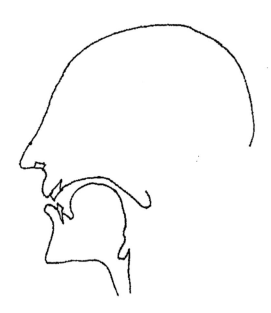

/u/ as in do

Description of production of sound. The lips are rounded. The tongue is arched high in the back of the mouth. Vocalized air is expelled over the tongue and out the mouth. The resulting sound should be /u/ as in do.

Description of articulators in diagram. The lips are rounded. The tongue is arched high in the back of the mouth.

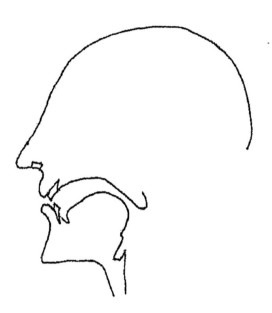

/ʊ/ as in book

Description of production of sound. The lips are rounded and protrude out slightly. The tongue is pulled back in the mouth. Vocalized air is expelled out of the mouth. The resulting sound should be /ʊ/ as in book.

Description of articulators in diagram. The lips are rounded and protrude out slightly. The tongue is pulled back in the mouth.

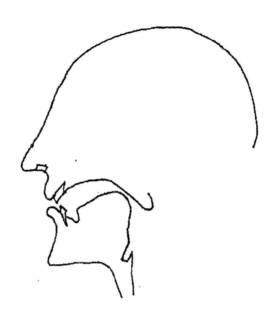

41

/ɔ/ as in author

Description of production of sound. The lips are well rounded. The tongue is back and low in the mouth with an elevation at the back of the tongue. Vocalized air is expelled over the tongue and out of the mouth. The resulting sound should be /ɔ/ as in author.

Description of articulators in diagram. The lips are well rounded. The tongue is back and low in the mouth with an elevation at the back of the tongue.

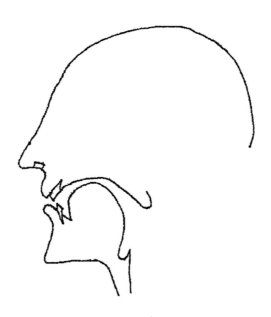

43

/ε/ as in he͟lp

Description of production of sound. The lips are unrounded. The tongue is pushed forward and relatively relaxed. Vocalized air is expelled over the tongue and out the mouth. The resulting sound should be /ε/ as in he͟lp.

Description of articulators in diagram. The lips are unrounded. The tongue is pushed forward and relatively relaxed.

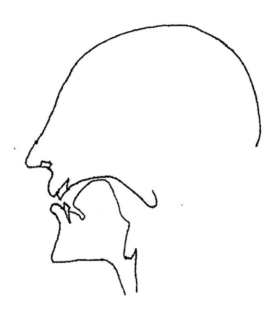

45

/ae/ as in b<u>a</u>t

Description of production of sound. The lips are unrounded. The
tongue is flat and flaccid on the bottom of the mouth. Vocalized air is
expelled over the tongue and out of the mouth. The resulting sound
should be /ae/ as in b<u>a</u>t.

Description of articulators in diagram. The lips are unrounded. The
tongue is flat and flaccid on the bottom of the mouth.

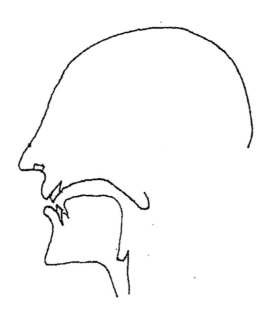

47

/eɪ/ as in <u>at</u>e

Description of production of sound. The mouth is open. The tongue is pushed forward and is slightly tense. Vocalized air produces the air at the front of the mouth. The resulting sound should be /eɪ/ as in <u>at</u>e.

Description of articulators in diagram. The mouth is open. The tongue is pushed forward and is slightly tense.

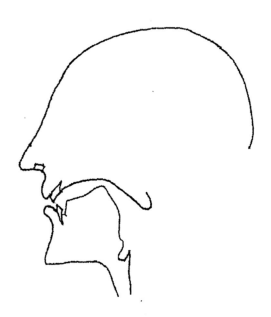

49

/aI/ as in sky_

Description of production of sound. The mouth is open wide and the lips are unrounded. The tongue is moved to a high front position. Vocalized air is expelled out of the mouth. The resulting sound should be /aI/ as in sky.

Description of articulators in diagram. The mouth is open wide and the lips are unrounded. The tongue is moved to a high front position.

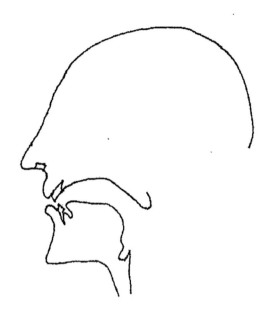

51

/ɔI/ as in bo_y

Description of production of sound. The lips are slightly rounded. The tongue moves from a low back to a high front in a gliding motion. Vocalized air is expelled out of the mouth. The resulting sound should be /ɔI/ as in bo_y.

Description of articulators in diagram. The lips are slightly rounded. The tongue moves from a low back to a high front in a gliding motion.

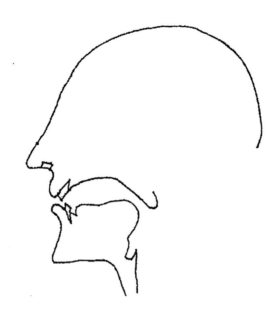

/oʊ/ as in open

Description of production of sound. The lips are well rounded. The tongue is pulled back and the mouth is taunt. Vocalized air is expelled over the tongue and out of the mouth. The resulting sound should be /oʊ/ as in open.

Description of articulators in diagram. The lips are well rounded. The tongue is pulled back and the mouth is taunt.

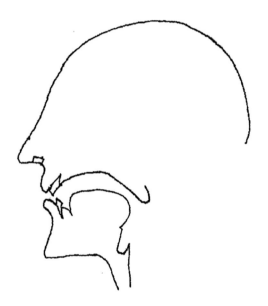

55

/aʊ/ as in c<u>o</u> w

Description of production of sound. The lips are rounded. The tongue moves from a low front to a high back with the tongue remaining relaxed. Vocalized air is expelled out of the mouth. The resulting sound should be /aʊ/ as in c<u>o</u> w.

Description of articulators in diagram. The lips are rounded. The tongue moves froma low front to a high back with the tongue remaining relaxed.

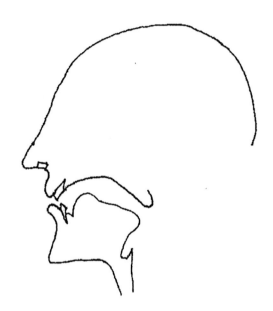

/ʌ/ as in fu̲n

Description of production of sound. The mouth is open wide and the lips are unrounded. Raise the midsection of the tongue and keep it tense. Vocalized air is expelled out of the mouth. The resulting sound should be /ʌ/ as in fu̲n.

Description of articulators in diagram. The mouth is open wide and the lips are unrounded. Raise the midsection of the tongue and keep it tense.

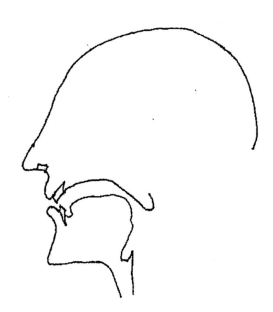

/ə/ as in alone

Description of production of sound. The lips are unrounded. The tongue is pulled back and raised in the middle. Vocalized air is expelled out of the mouth. The resulting sound should be /ə/ as in alone.

Description of articulators in diagram. The lips are unrounded. The tongue is pulled back and raised in the middle.

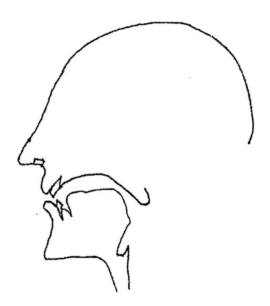

/ɝ/ as in b<u>ir</u>d

Description of production of sound. The lips are unrounded. The tongue is raised in the middle with the tip of the tongue pressed flat. Vocalized air is expelled out of the mouth. The resulting sound should be /ɝ/ as in b<u>ir</u>d .

Description of articulators in diagram. The lips are unrounded. The tongue is raised in the middle with the tip of the tongue pressed flat.

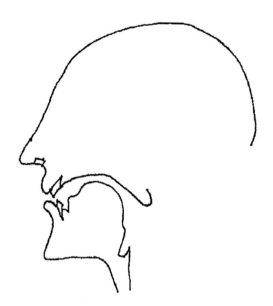

/ə/ as in nev<u>e r</u>

Description of production of sound. The lips are unrounded. The tongue is raised in the middle of the mouth. Vocalized air is expelled out of the mouth. The resulting sound should be /ə/ as in nev<u>er</u>.

Description of articulators in diagram. The lips are unrounded. The tongue is raised in the middle of the mouth.

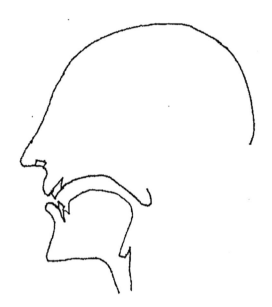

Chapter 8

Diagnostic

Even though the Priority Method uses a map of transfer errors that occur from the L1 to the L2, each ESL student will have their own specific errors. Before errors can be corrected they must be realized and diagnosed. This is where diagnostic testing is essential for preliminary evaluation of transfer errors in the ESL student. The diagnostic test consists of a tape recording device, blank tapes and material written in English. The ESL student is to read aloud into the tape recording device the written material, made up of English words and sentences, at a normal cadence. The ESL student will then read the same material aloud at a faster pace and again at a slower pace than normal.

The increase and decrease of reading speed will stress the student and give a more accurate body of data than data at a normal rate of speed alone. Because the readings have a transcript, the original material that was read, there is a correspondence with the recorded material. By playing back the tape of the students English readings, an accurate body of sound production can be evaluated for phonetic quality, stress and intonation. By marking on a copy of the transcript of the material what errors occurred and where those errors occurred within the context of the sound pattern, a detailed analysis of these errors can be deduced. Once a record of these errors is made then the process of correcting them can commence.

Because there is both a record of errors as well as a copy of these errors, the diagnostic tape, these can be used as guide posts for evaluating improvements in the ESL student over time. An important note in choosing English reading material for the diagnostic test. Because the diagnostic test is to test pronunciation rather than competency of reading skills, the material used should be cognitively accessible to the ESL student and relatively comfortable to read aloud at a normal rate of speed.

Summary

The major emphases of the Priority Method is the prioritizing of common transitional errors in ESL students. Efficiency, speed and accuracy are all the results of utilizing the Priority Method. The Priority Method allows for efficient removal of pronunciation errors in all ESL students and although allows for a clear and logical progression for the student to follow, it is of little use if the ESL student does not follow the instructions or make an attempt to constantly analyze their speech and listening skills away from the lessons. Only by continuous practice and awareness can the methods employed by the Priority Method serve to aid the ESL student in improving their speech.

Appendix

Pacific Language Institute
P.O. Box 2214
Cupertino, CA 95015-2214

Bradley S. Tice
Director

An Abstract of The Priority Method
on the Phonetics of the ESL Student

The Priority Method evolved from theories from first and second language acquisition and child language development. Along with error analysis theories , technical advances in equipment have allowed the Priority Method to offer a complete language diagnostic, analysis and training format. Its significant variation from all previous SLA pedagogy is that it concentrates on areas of weakness, prioritizing common areas of transitional errors from L1 to L2 , that commonly occur in the phonetic production and delivery of the ESL student , and focuses on the key areas that have significant sociolinguistic and linguistic effects on the ESL student. Why priorities errors over other aspects of second language learning? Because errors are the significant areas where the student's self confidence and progress come into play. Because negative aspects in any or all of the above will impede and/or stigmatize the ESL student and can be a major factor in having the student quit.

Many errors are common to each ESL language group, giving that group a preliminary map of errors that can be expected before the student arrives at that point. The specific phonetic area covered will be common consonant and vowel errors in the ESL student. There will be a text, work book and a tape of which the work book and tape will interact with each other using the Priority Method and a Learning Loop. The Learning Loop is a term that describes the learning system used to facilitate the correct recognition and production of the English sound pattern. It uses two tape recorders of which one is to play the tape with the exercises on it of a Model of English pronunciation. The second tape recorder is recording both the Model pronunciation and the students attempt to duplicate the Model English sound pattern. Because the student hears only those sound patterns that are similar or the same to their L1 language the need to compare their L2 production of English with that of a Model of English will result in a more accurate diagnosis. The potential of this method as a supplement to any language course or program is great as it can be used with any language group and at any level of learning.

The Priority Method

Bradley S. Tice

The Priority Method is a three step system designed to evaluate, diagnose, and correct phonemic transfer errors from the L1 to the L2 in SLA, Second Language Acquisition, students and will focus on Polish students learning ESL. The term Priority Method was used because the process prioritizes phonemic transfer errors over other aspects of the sound system and deals only with those aspects of the sound pattern that are alien to the SLA student's L1. The reason for this is two fold as, (a) why spend time with all of the sound pattern when only a fraction will be effected, and (b) by focusing on only those areas of weakness in the overall sound pattern, the transfer errors, a more efficient use of time and energy can be spent on correcting these errors.

By decreasing the overall time of acquiring this aspect of pronunciation, the motivation to learn the new language will be high as correct pronunciation will promote an increase in the use of the spoken L2, (George:1972), and this builds a strong foundation for future rewards in learning the L2.

Step One

The first step of The Priority Method is the evaluation of transfer errors that occur from the L1 to the L2 in SLA students and is done by the use of Contrastive Analysis. This hypothesis proposed by Lado in 1957, (Felix:1980), maintains that the L2 is acquired by these elements most similar to the L1. Thus those elements that are similar from the L1 to the L2 will provide a common phonemic map of transfer errors. This is the theory behind the use of contrastive analysis. The content of the language problems are the transfer errors from the L1 to the L2. The phonology of the SLA student is used as a bases from which a phonemic evaluation of the L2 can take place. From this evaluation, a common distribution of errors is made and can be the starting point of error correction. The use of Contrastive Analysis as a preliminary map of transfer errors is a solid foundation from which to build a general map of transfer errors as the L1 has influence on the L2 as confirmed by Dulay, Burt and Krashen (1982). Because each SLA student is different, individual testing of their respect sound pattern quality is done by the use of Error Analysis.

Step Two

The second part of the Priority Method is the use of Error

Analysis as a diagnostic system used to identify all sound pattern errors, including phonological ones, but is used in this case to expose phonemic transfer errors in SLA students. The SLA student is given a brief, one page, sample text written in the L2 and is to read this text aloud into a tape recording device. The sample text is designed to test the SLA student's level of pronunciation and is not a reading test. The sample text should be read with some ease by the student to make the use of such an L2 text valid. The tape can then be played to diagnose all sound pattern errors and used against the sample text for reference. The sample text and tape recording should be saved for future reference in evaluating the student's pronunciation performance as the same sample text should be used as a control factor in these diagnostic tests.

Step Three

The third and final step of The Priority Method is the correction of these pronunciation errors evaluated and diagnosed in steps one and two of The Priority Method. This process is done with the use of a Language Learning Loop which is the incorporation of an input-output system of language feedback. Two tape recorders are used of which the (a) tape recorder is playing a model of the L2 sound pattern while, simultaneously, the (b) tape recorder is recording both the model L2 sound and the

pronunciation attempts by the SLA student to model their sound

pattern quality with that of the (a) tape recorder model of sound

of the L2.

This closed system of communication, as described by Shannon

and Weaver (1949), is designed to give the SLA student

viable feedback in the manner of ideal pronunciation, the (a) tape

recording of a model of the L2, and feedback from the SLA

student's pronunciation attempts and the model of the L2. The

SLA student then has a model to compare and contrast the

pronunciation attempts with that of an ideal model of the L2

sound pattern. This process of feedback, Perren and Trim (1971),

of the model and student attempt of the L2, especially the

sensori-motor process in articulation, is essential in acquiring

the correct model of the spoken L2.

Materials
    Materials for The Priority Method are designed around two

areas of practice: (a) routinized oral practice that is developed

from simple, phoneme, to complex, sentences, and (b) articulation

practice with diagrams and explanations. The routinized oral

practice is the heart of the process of correction and is used with the Language Learning Loop to provide feedback and offer comparative and contrastive analysis by the use of a model of the L2. Although the term 'routine' has negative implications in current ESL thinking, see (Richards and Rogers:1986), it is still the most ideal process of training the articulators and hearing of the SLA student. Redundancy, repetition, occurs at three places, (George:1972), in the input model of communication. Redundancy at the information source, when a statement is repeated. The second is the natural redundancy inherent in the code, the repetition in the phonology of a language. And the third redundancy is information already at the information destination.

The information source, speaker, redundancy is done to make the signal, message, clear for the receiver, listener, and that is why it is repeated. The output mode of the process is the reverse of the previous communication model. The listener, once decoded and processed the message, will become the information source with the desired, hopefully, response. This is what the student is evaluated on. Repetition of the information source signal, message, by the student is to facilitate correct pronunciation and usage of the spoken L2.

The material is designed around the hierarchical premise of simple to complex with the phoneme being the smallest unit of sound and the sentence being the most advanced. The SLA student is given a list of L2 words and sentences that incorporate the transfer error phonemes into words and sentences from which to practice the L2 sound pattern. The use of articulation practice to define the physiological processes of pronunciation are done by the use of articulatory diagrams and explained sound stream control. The diagrams of articulators are usually mid-saggital diagrams of human heads exposing ideal articulation points for each sound unit. Explanations of sound stream control, voicing and breath, are also an advantage for the SLA student to know and can be combined with articulation practice.

Samples
     The following are a sample list of transfer errors most likely to be found in Polish ESL students. The transfer errors and substitutions are taken from Swan and Smith (1987), Retman (1961), and Lyra (1962). The bracketed symbols are IPA.
(a) The vowel [a] as in hot will be substituted for [o].
(b) The vowel [ŋ] as in sing will be substituted for [en].
(c) The consonant [t] as in tan will be substituted for [d].
(d) The consonant [h] as in hat will be substituted for [x].

(e) The consonant [k] as in <u>keep</u> will be substituted for [x].

This is just a sampling of transfer errors and individual student errors may differ. This is why the second step of The Priority Method is designed to access individual errors in SLA students.

Conclusion

The Priority Method offers a systematic process of phonemic transfer evaluation, diagnoses and correction that can be used with all languages and at all levels of second language acquisition. It must be stressed that The Priority Method only deals with phonemic, rather than phonological, properties of sound and is not a phonological method as it does not deal with language stress and intonation.

The Priority Method can be a useful tool in correcting the often lingering effects of phonemic transfer errors that have become a 'characterization' of learning a new language as best depicted in Ross's (1937) literary works. The average duration of The Priority Method if used four times a week one hour each day for three to four months. Once the transfer and individual errors are correct in the SLA student the need for The Priority Method becomes redundant as the method has worked.

References

Dulay, H., Burt, M., & Krashen, S. (1982). Language two. New York: Oxford University Press.

Felix, S.W. (1980). Second language development. Tubingen: Gunter Narr Verlag.

George, H.V. (1972). Common errors in language learning. Massachusetts: Newbury House Publishers.

Lado, R. (1961). Language testing. London: Longman.

Lyra, F. (1962). English and polish in contact. Unpublished doctoral dissertation, Indiana University.

Perren, G.E., & Trim, J.L.M. (1971). Applications of linguistics. Cambridge: Cambridge University Press.

Retman, R. (1961). Predicting difficulties of polish students of english and of english students of polish from comparison of sequential phonemes in both languages. Unpublished master's thesis, Georgetown University.

Richards, J. C., & Rogers, T.S. (1986). Approaches and methods in language teaching. Cambridge: Cambridge University Press.

Ross, L.Q. (1937). The education of hyman kaplan. New York: Harcourt, Brace and Company.

Shannon, C. & Weaver, W. (1949). The mathematical theory of communication. Urbana: University of Illinois Press.

Swan, M., & Smith, B. (1987). Learner english: a teacher's guide to interference and other problems. Cambridge: Cambridge University Press.

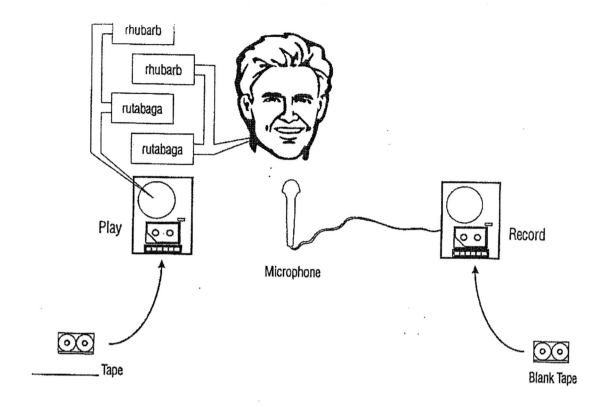

rhubarb

rhubarb

rutabaga

rutabaga

Play

Microphone

Record

Tape

Blank Tape

A

rhubarb

rhubarb

rutabaga

rutabaga

Off

Rewind
and
Play

B

81

Bradley S. Tice, Director
Pacific Language Institute
P.O. Box 2214
Cupertino, CA 95015-2214
U.S.A.
Business Telephone# (408)253-4449

THE INTERNATIONAL PHONETIC ALPHABET (revised to 1993)

CONSONANTS (PULMONIC)

	Bilabial	Labiodental	Dental	Alveolar	Postalveolar	Retroflex	Palatal	Velar	Uvular	Pharyngeal	Glottal
Plosive	p b			t d		ʈ ɖ	c ɟ	k g	q ɢ		ʔ
Nasal	m	ɱ		n		ɳ	ɲ	ŋ	N		
Trill	B			r					R		
Tap or Flap				ɾ		ɽ					
Fricative	ɸ β	f v	θ ð	s z	ʃ ʒ	ʂ ʐ	ç ʝ	x ɣ	χ ʁ	ħ ʕ	h ɦ
Lateral fricative				ɬ ɮ							
Approximant		ʋ		ɹ		ɻ	j	ɰ			
Lateral approximant				l		ɭ	ʎ	L			

Where symbols appear in pairs, the one to the right represents a voiced consonant. Shaded areas denote articulations judged impossible.

CONSONANTS (NON-PULMONIC)

Clicks		Voiced implosives		Ejectives	
ʘ	Bilabial	ɓ	Bilabial	ʼ	as in:
ǀ	Dental	ɗ	Dental/alveolar	pʼ	Bilabial
ǃ	(Post)alveolar	ʄ	Palatal	tʼ	Dental/alveolar
ǂ	Palatoalveolar	ɠ	Velar	kʼ	Velar
ǁ	Alveolar lateral	ʛ	Uvular	sʼ	Alveolar fricative

SUPRASEGMENTALS

ˈ	Primary stress	ˌfoʊnəˈtɪʃən
ˌ	Secondary stress	
ː	Long	eː
ˑ	Half-long	eˑ
˘	Extra-short	ĕ
.	Syllable break	ɹi.ækt
|	Minor (foot) group	
‖	Major (intonation) group	
‿	Linking (absence of a break)	

TONES & WORD ACCENTS

LEVEL		CONTOUR	
e̋ or ꜛ	Extra high	ě or ꜛ	Rising
é ꜝ	High	ê ꜞ	Falling
ē ꜓	Mid	e᷄ ꜗ	High rising
è ꜔	Low	e᷅ ꜘ	Low rising
ȅ ꜕	Extra low	e᷈ ꜖	Rising-falling
ꜜ	Downstep	↗	Global rise
ꜛ	Upstep	↘	Global fall

etc.

VOWELS

Where symbols appear in pairs, the one to the right represents a rounded vowel.

OTHER SYMBOLS

ʍ	Voiceless labial-velar fricative	ɕ ʑ	Alveolo-palatal fricatives
w	Voiced labial-velar approximant	ɺ	Alveolar lateral flap
ɥ	Voiced labial-palatal approximant	ɧ	Simultaneous ʃ and x
ʜ	Voiceless epiglottal fricative		
ʢ	Voiced epiglottal fricative	Affricates and double articulations can be represented by two symbols joined by a tie bar if necessary.	
ʡ	Epiglottal plosive	k͡p t͡s	

DIACRITICS

Diacritics may be placed above a symbol with a descender, e.g. ŋ̊

̥	Voiceless	n̥ d̥	̤	Breathy voiced	b̤ a̤	̪	Dental	t̪ d̪
̬	Voiced	s̬ t̬	̰	Creaky voiced	b̰ a̰	̺	Apical	t̺ d̺
ʰ	Aspirated	tʰ dʰ	̼	Linguolabial	t̼ d̼	̻	Laminal	t̻ d̻
̹	More rounded	ɔ̹	ʷ	Labialized	tʷ dʷ	̃	Nasalized	ẽ
̜	Less rounded	ɔ̜	ʲ	Palatalized	tʲ dʲ	ⁿ	Nasal release	dⁿ
̟	Advanced	u̟	ˠ	Velarized	tˠ dˠ	ˡ	Lateral release	dˡ
̠	Retracted	i̠	ˤ	Pharyngealized	tˤ dˤ	̚	No audible release	d̚
̈	Centralized	ë	̴	Velarized or pharyngealized	ɫ			
̽	Mid-centralized	̽e̽	̝	Raised	e̝ (ɹ̝ = voiced alveolar fricative)			
̩	Syllabic	l̩	̞	Lowered	e̞ (β̞ = voiced bilabial approximant)			
̯	Non-syllabic	e̯	̘	Advanced Tongue Root	e̘			
˞	Rhoticity	ə˞	̙	Retracted Tongue Root	e̙			

83

Language Learning Loop: A Feedback System

By Dr. Bradley S. Tice
Advanced Human Design
Cupertino, California U.S.A.

The Language Learning Loop is a feedback loop circuit employed to record, evaluate and correct speech sounds of both first and second language learners. The theory behind this system comes from the information sciences, specifically Shannon and Weaver's seminal work "The Mathematical Theory of Communication" published in 1949. Although behaviorism is used to 're-train' the articulators for modification purposes to a target norm of a social ideal of the sound production desired, the system itself is a systems engineering model of a mathematical model of a closed loop system of information signal transfer and modification.

A simple input/ output model of this system will give a general idea of how the language learning loop system functions. The first recording device is playing a model of the ideal sound production of that target language. The second recording device is recording not only the model of ideal production of the target language, but also the attempts of the student to match that target language production by repeating the ideal target models sound delivery (Tice, 1997).

1

84

From this recording of the model and the attempts to match the model sound production of the target language, a clear and straight-forward recording of the model and attempts of that model can be heard in a comparative and contrastive manner that is necessary for understanding and correction, to achieve the ideal target language production norms. It cannot be understated the importance of this closed loop model of feedback in the diagnosis, evaluation and correction properties this system has to offer the first and second language learning student.

From a systems engineering standpoint, the language learning loop is a self-contained system using existing technologies, tape-recorders, and can be easily implemented into a language laboratory environment, that has been around since the late 1950's, in most language schools or language departments around the world. In other words, this system has a very 'trivial' technology transfer problems inherent in it, and so, can be implemented with little or no costs to a existing language laboratory modules.

The language learning loop will be defined in terms of an information science model and practical aspects of the listening

2

and vocalization pathways will be analyzed for applications to the language learning student.

Diagrams of Language Learning Loop

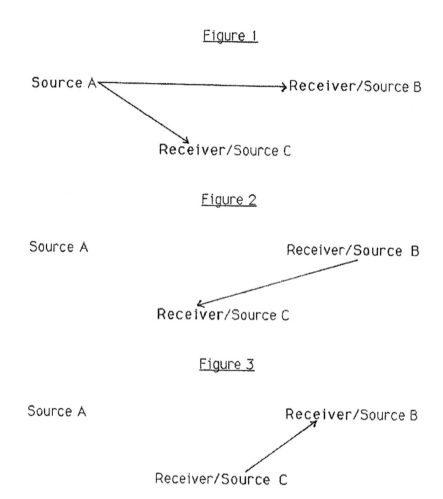

Figure 1

Source A ⟶ Receiver/Source B

Receiver/Source C

Figure 2

Source A   Receiver/Source B

Receiver/Source C

Figure 3

Source A   Receiver/Source B

Receiver/Source C

3

Key to Diagrams

Source A: Output tape recorder playing Target L2 sounds, then followed by spaces for L2 student's attempts to produce the L2 sounds.[1]

Receiver/Source B: Input functions as a receiver, the L2 student listens to the Target L2 sound. Output functions as a source, the L2 student produces an attempt of the L2 sound.

Receiver/ Source C: Input function #1 as a receiver, records Target L2 sound. Input Function #2 as a receiver, records the L2 students attempt to produce the L2 sound. Output functions as a source, play recorded Target L2 and the L2 students attempt to produce the L2 sound.

Note: The goal of this system is the Output mode of the Receiver/Source C as it affords a comparative/contrastive analysis of the L2 sound system.

Information Theory to Language Learning Loop

The communication model for human speech found in Shannon and Weaver's seminal work <u>The Mathematical Theory of</u>

---

[1] L2 is a linguistic notation for second language, i.e. all languages learned after the first language..

Communication has for almost 50 years been the bench mark for describing human communication (Shannon and Weaver, 1949). This model is considered the most 'influential' model of communication ever and with the inclusion of a unidirectional arrow, accounts for a feedback system inherent in human communication transmissions (Pearce, 1994: 20). A model of this linear diagram can be found in Figure A.

<u>Figure A</u>

Source — Encoding — Message — Decoding — Receiver

The importance of information theory to the language learning loop is the robustness of the method, in both the mathematical and diagrammatic forms, to explain the system accurately with minimal entropy to the concepts being conveyed. This has been accepted as a standard for the past 50 years and the novelty of such a descriptive system to carry information on complex human behavior and modify and reduce it to a series of arrows and block diagrams, without any major loss of content to the core information base, is still an amazing feature of information theory. Fifty years later and this method of analysis to describe systems is still the paradigm to beat.

5

References

1. Pearce, W.B. Interpersonal Communication: Making Social Worlds. New York: HarperCollins College Publishers, 1994.

2. Shannon, C.E. and Weaver, W. The Mathematical Theory of Communication. Urbana: University of Illinois Press, 1949.

3. Tice, B.S. "Language Learning Loop: A Pronunciation System for Japanese ESL". TESOL MATTERS, Volume 7, Number 2, April/May 1997.

6

Reference

Reference List

1.   Comrie, B.(1990). The World's Major Languages.
     Oxford: Oxford University Press.

2.   Evans, B W.(1976). Improving Your Speech "Here's How".
     Iowa: Kendall/Hunt Publishing Company.

3.   Haycraft, B.(1978). The Teaching of Pronunciation: A Classroom
     Guide. London: Longman.

4.   Jung, M.W.(1962). "A Contrastive Study of English and Korean Segmental
     Phonemes with Some Suggestions Toward Pedogogical Application."
     M.S. Georgetown University.

5.   Kenworthy, J.(1988).Teaching English Pronunciation.
     London: Longman.

6.   Lilly-Cheng, L.R.(1987). Assessing Asian Language Performance.
     Rockville: Aspen Publishers Inc.

7.   Lindfors, J. W.(1987).Children's Language and Learning.
     New Jersey: Prentice-Hall, Inc.

8.   Richards, J. C. and T.S. Rodgers (1986).Approaches and Methods in
     Language Teaching: A Description and Analysis.
     Cambridge: Cambridge University Press.

9.   Roach, P.(1983).English Phonetics and Phonology.
     Cambridge: Cambridge University Press.

10. Swan, M. and B. Smith.(1987).Learner English: A Teacher's Guide to
     Interference and Other Problems. Cambridge: Cambridge University
     Press.

11. Tice, B. (1994, February). The priority method. Conference conducted at
     the 19th Annual CABE in San Jose, California.

13. Tiffany, W. R. and J. Carrel.(1977).Phonetics: Theory and Application..
     New York: McGraw-Hill.

Bradley S. Tice

About the Author

Dr. Tice is Director and Institute Professor of Language and Linguistics at the Pacific Language Institute located in Cupertino, California U.S.A. His primary interest is in language acquisition, bilingualism and aspects of phonology. He is a member of the following organizations: American Chemical Society, American Society for Microbiology, Association for Computing Machinery, I.E.E.E., The American Physical Society, American Institute of Aeronautics and Astronautics, the Committee on Space Research (COSPAR), California Association for Health, Physical Education, Recreation, and Dance, the Rocky Mountain Modern Language Association, and a founding member of The Mars Society. Dr. Tice has had previous affiliations with both the Stanford Linear Accelerator Center, Menlo Park, California U.S.A. and the NASA Ames Research Center, Moffett Field, California U.S.A. Dr. Tice is listed in the 26th edition of Marquis Who's Who in the West, 53rd Edition of Marquis Who's Who in America, and the 16th Edition of Marquis Who's Who in the World. Dr. Tice is also Director and Institute Professor of Chemistry at Advanced Human Design in Cupertino, California U.S.A. and CEO of Tice Pharmaceuticals in San Jose, California U.S.A.

Printed in the United States
114662LV00003B/57/A